Irish Traveller Women in London

a Celebration of History and Culture

by

Tish Collins & Ally Ward

an LIWC publication 2010

First published by the London Irish Women's Centre,
59 Stoke Newington Church Street, London N16 0AR

www.liwc.co.uk

© Tish Collins and LIWC 2010

All rights reserved.
Without limiting the rights under copyright reserved above, no part of this publication may be reproduced, stored in or introduced into a retrieval system, or transmitted, in any form or by any means (electronic, mechanical, photocopying, recording or otherwise), without the prior written permission of the publisher.

ISBN 978-0-9521522-6-2

Acknowledgements

The exhibition and this book were made possible by the kind loan of photographs, artefacts and other materials by Ms Ally Ward and her family.

This book was produced with assistance from the Irish Government Emigrant Support Advisory Committee, for which we are most grateful.

Typesetting and design - Caroline Foulkes

CONTENTS

Foreword by Tish Collins   2

1: Where do Travellers come from?   4
    Discrimination, Marginalisation

2: Culture   13
    Education and Ambition, Religion, Marriage, Food, Daily Routines, Caravans, Living in a house compared with on a site.

3: London Irish Women's Centre   35
    Vision, Mission, Strategic Aims, LIWC Case Studies using the Human Rights Act, Typical Issues, LIWC Case Study of Ms C.

4: Legislation   42

Appendix 1: Definition of Ethnicity   50
Appendix 2: Irish Travellers recognised as a   51
               Legal Ethnicity
Appendix 3: International Law   52
Appendix 4: Site Provision   54

Foreword

This book was written to accompany the London Irish Women's Centre Exhibition held in June 2010 as a contribution towards the 3rd Gypsy, Roma and Traveller History Month. Our display depicting travelling through time including a walk-through caravan, was mounted by the exhibition team of Ally Ward, Angelina Ward, Caroline Foulkes, Bernie Whelan, Nick Newland and Tish Collins.

I would like to thank LIWC's regular service users, visitors and our Advice and Counselling staff who showed great forbearance whilst the exhibition was under construction – especially with a man working in the building for best part of three weeks.

We are most grateful to the Irish Government Emigrant Support Programme which has been a significant supporter of our work for many years and without whom this book would not have been published.

The London Irish Women's Centre (LIWC) was established in 1983 to address the needs of marginalised and excluded Irish women in London and has been a haven of creativity and free expression for Irish women for over a quarter of a century.

LIWC delivers a comprehensive culturally sensitive service for women of Irish and Irish Traveller birth or descent tailored to individual needs. We have a safe women-only Centre in Stoke Newington and provide outreach and home visits as required.

LIWC is committed to empowering Irish women and their families and seeks to offer an holistic service and the most practical support.

Chapter 2: *Culture* is based on interviews conducted in recent months by LIWC and reflects personal views of a number of Irish Traveller women.

Chapter 4: *London Irish Women's Centre* reflects some of the work undertaken at the Centre; we are grateful to Arlene Kilim, Advice Co-ordinator at LIWC for her tireless and tenacious enthusiasm and for providing the case studies (which have been edited to protect individuals).

We are delighted to be able to mount this exhibition celebrating Irish Traveller history and culture and to give some insight into the life of women Travellers in particular.

Tish Collins
Director, London Irish Women's Centre

[1]

Where do Travellers come from?

Travelling people have lived in Britain for centuries and the main groups are of Irish, Romani, English or East European origin. Irish Travellers make up the majority of the Travelling population in London, drawn by the same economic pressures which have attracted the settled Irish community over the years.

Some Irish Travellers call themselves Minceirs or Pavees and can trace their history back to pre-Christian times.

Their language Shelta has two main dialects, Gammon and Cant, which have been used for over 800 years.

The Irish and Scottish Travellers known as the Nawkins or Cairds are said to be descended from the Ancient Picts – the earliest known inhabitants of Ireland and most of Scotland.

At various stages in history enclosures, land evictions and famine forced more people onto the road to look for work and food.

Irish Travellers originate from trades people who for centuries earned a living travelling from area to area helping with the harvest and other agricultural work, breeding and trading horses or making tin pots and pans for settled households.

It is from this latter activity that the term Tinker derives, once quite acceptable to Travellers but now considered derogatory.

Some English and Welsh travellers call themselves Gypsies or Romanichals and originate from India. In Tudor Times, the time of Shakespeare, these Travellers were called *Egyptians* as some had travelled through Egypt – hence the term Gypsy.

Other Traveller groups claim their cultural heritage back to the nomadic metal workers who followed the Roman Army into Britain.

In more recent years so called "New Age" Travellers have appeared, mainly emerging from the festival scene.

Ethnic Travellers share a distinct ideology, one aspect of which is closely associated with a tradition of travelling nomadism.

"We move not to be strangers but because it's our way; it's the freedom to get up and go".

"In the Traveller way of life, people come before property or financial value. We look at the person themselves rather than what they look like or what they have."
[Quotes from Bridget Gaffey: Moving Stories, 1992 p9]

There is an ideological clash between the Traveller way of life and that of a society based upon individualism and home ownership.

Throughout history Travellers have faced hostile legislation and discrimination from the rest of society. Efforts have been made to restrict the travelling lifestyle in Britain from the 16th century, Tudor times, up to the present day. Along with Jews, trade unionists and communists, Gypsies were a significant target for the Nazi death camps in Europe between 1933 and 1945.

Since the 1980's Travellers have been recognised as an ethnic minority in Britain and thus, with the exception of "New Age" travellers, are protected under the Race Relations Act 1976.

Modern technology has transformed the Traveller way of life and they continue to experience institutionalised discrimination and prejudice.

The use of machines in agriculture in post-1945 Britain meant much of the traditional seasonal work carried out by Travellers in rural communities no longer existed. The introduction of plastic and enamel goods reduced demand for tin-ware items traditionally produced by Travellers. Increases in car ownership and changes in shopping habits (including Pound Shops) limited the demand for household goods and small trinkets traditionally made and sold door-to-door by Traveller women and children.

These changes led to widespread migration to towns and cities where Travellers faced economic and social marginalisation.

Today's urban Traveller men in paid employment are likely to be self-employed and take up casual work in construction, scrap dealing, laying tarmac on roads or painting and decorating. Some are market traders. Traveller women have the main responsibility for bringing up the children.

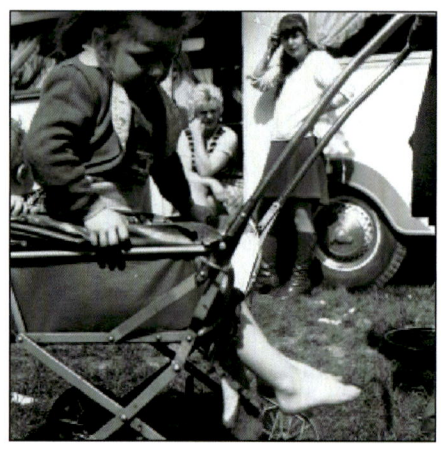

Some Travellers have established successful businesses but the majority live on low incomes and many are dependent on state benefits.

Discrimination

Various discriminatory laws which have severely reduced the number of stopping places available have made matters even more difficult for Travellers. Many have had to settle on static sites (where available) or move into houses. This proves difficult for parents but also children who are brought up with family stories of travelling and yearn to experience it for themselves.

Irish Travellers in Britain have suffered discrimination and racism both as Travellers and as Irish people. Before the 1980's, Irish Travellers were, in the main, excluded from official sites and, with the exception of the Westway site in Hammersmith, there were virtually no Irish travellers on official sites in London before 1983.

The Westway site, Hammersmith London

The *"No Irish"* and *"No blacks, no dogs, no Irish"* signs that were prevalent in the 1940's and 50's barring people from accommodation and shops, did disappear but *"No Traveller"* signs continued into the 1990's.

'No Travellers served in this shop'

In 2005 *The Sun* newspaper conducted a racist campaign against travellers and, despite complaints to the Press Complaints Commission no action was taken against *The Sun*. There have been studies which show local media campaigns have a direct correlation to local hostility.

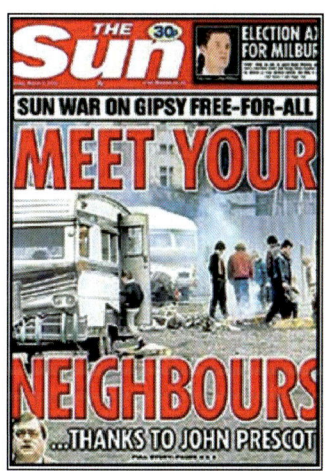

Marginalisation

In 2006 the Commission for Racial Equality (CRE) estimated there were between 200,000 and 300,000 Gypsies and Travellers in Britain – of which some 200,000 were living in housing. They also stated that *"Recent reports and evidence indicate that Irish Travellers are one of the most marginalised groups in society"*.

Irish in common with other Traveller groups fare the worst of any ethnic group in terms of health and education. Life expectancy for adults is at least 10 years less than the English average of 77 for males and 81 for females. Official statistics from Ireland indicate that the birth rate of Irish Travellers has decreased since the 1990s, but they still have one of the highest birth rates in Europe. The birth rate for the Traveller community for the year 2005 was 33.32 per 1000, possibly the highest birth rate recorded for any community in Europe.

By comparison, the Irish National Average was 15.0 in 2007.

In Ireland there are on average 10 times more driving fatalities within the Traveller community. At 22%, this represents the most common cause of death among Traveller males.

Roughly 10 times more infants die under the age of two, while a third of Travellers die before the age of 25. In addition, 80% of Travellers die before the age of 65. In Ireland, 2.6% of all deaths in the total population were for people aged under 25, versus 32% for the Travellers. Some 10% of Traveller children die before their second birthday, compared to just 1% of the general population. According to Van Cleemput et al (2004) Gypsy and Traveller women are 20 times more likely than other mothers to experience the death of a child.

According to the Department for Education and Skills in 2003 less than one quarter of Irish Traveller and Gypsy children obtained 5 GCSE A-C grades, compared with the national average of just over half.

The Department for Communities and Local Government published data indicating that one-third of caravan dwelling Gypsies and Irish Travellers do not have a legal or secure place to live. One-third live on unauthorised encampments. (See Appendix 4, p54)

[2]

Culture

This chapter is based on interviews conducted by LIWC.

Among Travelling peoples there is a strong sense of community, a firm belief in family values and an important awareness of and acknowledgment of belonging to an ancient culture.

Most Travellers, whether they are on the road or living in houses or on sites are conscious of having a long shared history of travelling life. They also share many cultural traditions and values which are passed on from generation to generation.

Today Irish Travellers share many customs which are noticeably nomadic and yet distinctly Irish in nature.

According to the Council of Europe in 1987:
"Travelling is more a state of mind than an actual situation. Its existence and importance are frequently more psychological than geographical. The Traveller, who loses all hope of ever setting off again or the possibility of doing so, also loses his identity as a Traveller."

There are traditional roles for women and men, which still largely dominate family life. The woman's role is to stay at home, bring up the children, keep the home clean and cook. Girls learn from their mothers and help rear their younger siblings by getting them washed and dressed in the mornings or helping at meal times.

Children will have a strong sense of right and wrong instilled in them from an early age.

The role of men is to provide for their family and teach work skills to their sons, taking them out to do a full day working on roofs, collecting and dealing scrap metal or laying tarmac, for example.

Fairs are an important part of the Irish and English Traveller calendar, notably at Appleby, Cambridge, Epsom and Stow.

Many Travellers make their living by trading at such fairs which can date their origins back many hundreds of years. Here horses are bought and sold and stalls will sell traditional craft wares as well as the general household goods and clothes seen at any country fair. Men will also be selling hand-made horseboxes, trailers and horsey accessories.

Women will have stalls of Crown Derby china, Waterford Crystal, baby clothes, costume jewellery and shoes. Swarovski crystals are also sold, particularly for embellishing wedding veils.

The fairs will be set over one or two weeks with accompanying entertainment, discos and clubbing. As whole families and friends gather in their finery for the fair there will be some weddings arranged over the course of the week and it is not unusual for a man to plan a marriage proposal at the event.

Bare knuckle fights are another traditional feature as are horse races, especially at Epsom.

Education and Ambition

Work for Travellers used to be based on the seasonal demands of agriculture and skilled manual labour passed down from father to son over many generations. Today there is hardly any such work around and most jobs require paper qualifications which the majority of Travellers do not have. For this reason it is seen as increasingly important amongst the travelling community that children stay at school to learn to read and write to better themselves.

However, most Traveller children do not want to stay on at school beyond learning the basics. The reasons are complex but after the age of around 13 Traveller children seem to be subject to a lot of bullying at school for their different way of life and accents and they feel looked down upon by the settled community. Older Traveller children may also bully them and say they are wasting their time at school and encourage the younger boys to look for ways to earn some money.

Some reports say that girls leave school early because their parents don't want them to have sex education or to mix with boys (especially from a different culture). However, others say it is because they don't find school relevant to their lives and they are not learning anything.

The ambition of a typical 14 year old Traveller girl is to get married and she won't see how physics, French or maths has any part in that. Very few have the ambition to become a doctor or nurse or take up any kind of profession as the traditional roles for women in the home are so ingrained. A mother would traditionally want her daughter to be married and happy.

Educational establishments are also very inflexible. Very few schools feel able to embrace changes in the curriculum to introduce subjects that would be of practical use to young women preparing for marriage and motherhood - such as courses in hair, nails, childcare or cookery. Childcare qualifications would also help young women to get jobs because often they will have learned the necessary skills from rearing younger siblings but without a recognised qualification no one will employ them.

About 20 years ago grandmothers started encouraging their daughters to take part in the running of schools and nurseries which were set up on sites, often with help from charities. These provided a good preparation for the children later going off to local state (County) or Catholic schools.

The Traveller Education Service also plays an important part in helping women access schools and educational support for their children. Literacy was often a barrier to prevent mothers finding out what was available and filling in the relevant forms.

This service varies in quality from area to area and some schools are willing to be more flexible than others. There is a general lack of understanding of just how important births, deaths and marriages are to the community and their need to take children out of school sometimes for a few weeks to attend a family event back in Ireland or in Yorkshire for example is recorded as absent without permission.

More recently some jobs have become available in Traveller Education seeking to recruit Travellers who can talk to people on sites and encourage school attendance. Unfortunately there is still a tendency to use application forms that demand qualifications of degree level or at least 3 A Levels as a minimum requirement – which rules out most Travellers. Until the forms become more accessible and requirements flexible to take experience into account there is unlikely to be much progress.

Religion

Traditionally Irish Travellers would have been Roman Catholics. There have been a few priests, such as Father Daly who was known as the Travellers' Priest and he would go all round the country to perform ceremonies such as funerals, Christenings and marriages, making local arrangements and negotiating on behalf of the family.

Most of the Irish Traveller families in Britain came from Ireland and still have relatives there. Honouring the dead is an important part of Traveller culture and when they travel back for family gatherings most will also visit graves. Travellers have their own special undertakers in Ireland.

Travellers lead extremely hard lives, whether they live on a permanent site or have been forced by circumstances to move into a house. They struggle with unemployment, discrimination and restrictions on movement – this effectively denies the traditional role of men to be the "breadwinner" or the provider. There is much evidence of clinical depression in men and women of this community. Alcoholism and drug misuse is also, anecdotally, an unacknowledged but increasing problem.

Some have turned away form the additional misery this can bring and found solace in a new evangelical religion. There has been a spread of "born again" Christianity amongst Travellers and a move away from Catholicism, particularly among Irish and English Travellers living on local authority sites.

Marriage

The wedding day is considered by many to represent one of the best days of their lives, but for the young Traveller girl who has been dreaming and planning her wedding since she was at least 14 this is regarded as the pinnacle of her whole life.

There are still a majority of "match" weddings where the families agree sometimes years in advance which girl is to marry which boy. Once arrangements have been made the girl is kept under extremely strict conditions, she is not even allowed a mobile phone and cannot go out alone or meet up with her betrothed. If she breaks the rules her name will be destroyed and her family dishonoured.

No wedding invitations are sent but word gets around to the extended families by social networking activities such as Facebook and mobile phones.

All celebrations are big social events and families will travel great distances to be together for christenings, weddings, funerals, first communion and confirmation. Ceremonies are the ideal occasion to catch up with friends and family who may be living hundreds of miles away or in Ireland, to show off outfits and perhaps meet potential partners for the first time.

There is a fashion for huge, extravagant wedding dresses and celebrity style Cinderella coach and horses for the bride. There are dressmakers who specialise in Traveller wedding outfits, each dress being unique.

Shopping for wedding clothes is a great excitement for young women who order lavish made-to-measure outfits. In older times, young women would have become skilled at making their own clothes or adapting and embellishing things they bought.

Food

Irish Travellers in Britain today enjoy classic meals such as boiled bacon, cabbage, carrots and potatoes, stew and soda bread. Fry-up breakfasts include the Irish white and black pudding and very salty home-cured bacon. Traditionally these were nourishing meals which could be made in cast iron pots over an open fire – but work equally as well in a saucepan on a cooker. They could also be made to expand to feed whoever appeared at meal time. Apart from feeding their own and perhaps the children of family and neighbours, the women prepare enough food for anybody who might drop in – be they family, neighbours, friends or even strangers. Offering and sharing food is an important part of the Traveller culture.

In rural areas hunting for hares to eat and cook over an open fire is traditional and hare coursing is particularly a sport for English Travellers.

Ovens are used for roasting meat and vegetables and modern day travellers shop in supermarkets and local shops alongside the settled community.

Older Traveller women used to make very sweet rice puddings using evaporated milk –as a real treat for the children – there was never pocket money to buy sweets or fizzy drinks. Before legislation forced Travellers on to permanent sites and there was more travelling done in country areas, the old women used to beg or sell trinkets to priests' houses and colleges and be given food in exchange.

Daily Routines for Irish Traveller Women

The day is based around the needs of the children and it is traditional to have large families. So the woman must get the children up, washed, dressed and given breakfast before being taken to school.

Back home she must clean the caravan inside and out and prepare the food. Children are collected from school, the older girls helping their mothers feed the children then wash them and put them to bed.

There is no sense of leisure for the women and certainly not the fashionable "me time". Mothers would not have had manicures or their hair styled – there was neither time nor money.

Younger women when not helping with family chores have more time to concentrate on their appearance, chat with friends and plan for their big wedding day.

Caravans

Skilled men used to make the traditional Irish barrel-topped caravans which were painted in bright colours and had beautifully carved panels. Often paint brushes were made from human hair – for example the end of a daughter's plait. These caravans were pulled by horses and were relatively light-weight compared with English gypsy caravans and showmen's vans.

Most would have a little stove for heating and cooking but no sink. There was no room for a kitchen as such and most cooking and washing activity would take place outdoors using open fires. Tin smith work was skilled and valued for making cans to hold water as well as other pots and pans.

A newly restored wagon

In transit...

By the 1960's and 70's touring caravans pulled by cars or vans were available. Some resembled a standard holiday caravan in wide use in Britain whilst others were beautifully ornamented and used much chrome and cut glass.

Today as site living tends to be a more or less permanent address, static caravans are the norm. These are large, multi-roomed homes with all modern conveniences.

Living in a House compared with on a Site

On a Traveller site there is a constant flow of people around and everyone gets to know one another quickly. It is a sociable and welcoming culture. However, most Travellers in houses say they feel isolated and lonely, that they feel they can't communicate with non-Travellers and they find it difficult to communicate with Travellers on sites. They feel they have been dragged away from their culture and by choice most would not live in houses. These tensions can lead to nervous problems and depression.

The children tend to be unhappy for similar reasons and are frequently bullied at school. Whilst some children make friends among the settled community, some neighbours don't want their children mixing with travellers. On a site there will be many children able to play out together and this early socialisation is good for their development and ability to fit into primary school.

On sites, women will look after children for any woman in need, especially if there is illness or a death in the family. This natural support system is not generally available to such women in houses.

Legislation has stopped the right to travel and the freedom to pull into the wayside at will. Instead there has been a limited programme of site provision and an insistence that Travellers are registered onto a permanent site or move in to housing (see more in Appendix 4 p54) .

There are not enough sites in Britain and not enough pitches on those sites. This leads to overcrowding where two families are sharing one pitch and even more families having to move into settled housing. The tradition of having many children means there is an ever increasing demand for pitches. Often women fleeing domestic violence or wanting to move away from particular neighbours on sites find their only option is to move into rented housing.

Traveller Sites are, in the main, built by Local Authorities and conditions vary considerably across the country. Some are well equipped with good access to local schools, doctors and dentists but most tend to be on waste ground beside railway lines or major road systems where the air is poor, facilities minimal and access to shops difficult. Upkeep and repair of property, drains and communal areas or fences is also patchy. There is a feeling that there is discrimination against Irish Travellers and that some site management are not being fair. Consequently, tensions tend to build and occasionally flare up between the different cultures.

[3]
London Irish Women's Centre

Now in its 28th year, the London Irish Women's Centre (LIWC) has the following vision, mission and aims:

Vision
The London Irish Women's Centre exists to empower, inspire, mobilise and celebrate women of Irish birth and descent in London.

Mission Statement
London Irish Women's Centre:
- believes in promoting equality of opportunity for women of Irish birth and descent, regardless of their social and economic status, colour, religious, political or sexual orientation.
- believes in enabling women to recognise their own power and their ability to change their own lives.
- believes that Irish women have a distinct identity and culture and seeks to achieve a positive identity and status for Irish women in the Irish and the wider community.

- works to combat isolation and provide access to a safe and supportive community.
- believes in taking an holistic approach to the needs of Irish women.

Strategic Aims
- To provide and develop accessible, culturally competent services for marginalised Irish women in London, tailored to their individual needs.
- To target specifically disadvantaged groups of Irish women – Travellers, older women, women with mental and physical health problems, women in abusive situations and homeless women.
- To increase access to appropriate services by providing advice, information, advocacy and support.
- To develop cultural and social events for Irish women to enable them to form and access a welcoming and supportive community.
- To bring together Irish women from across London to formulate and address their own needs.
- To inform, influence and lead policy debates on gender, cultural identity, service provision and discrimination in all forms.

Highly qualified Advice staff deliver advice, advocacy and information on a range of issues including housing, welfare benefits, reviews, tribunal representation, debt, family issues, employment, pensions, tax credits, arriving from/returning to Ireland. Casework often exposes underlying issues including high levels of domestic violence, poverty, poor health, harassment, poor mental health. Because of its specialist nature, LIWC offers a greater degree of support than most mainstream agencies and also holds the

Community Legal Service Quality Mark for its work on welfare benefits, housing and debt. Internal referrals take place between LIWC's Advice and Counselling services and clients are also able to self-refer. For the past three years we have enjoyed a successful working partnership with Immigrant Counselling and Psychotherapy (icap), delivering services at our women-only Centre. LIWC is also a third party reporting centre for Hate Crime in Hackney and a referral agency for Hackney's Drug & Alcohol Team.

Our modest programme of group work, including a reminiscence group, helps break down barriers of isolation and there are plans for further groups development.

Group enjoying paper flower making at LIWC 25th anniversary event

LIWC Case Studies

The Human Rights Act: Changing Lives report published by the British institute of Human Rights in December 2008 to mark the 10th anniversary of the Act included some case studies from experience at the London Irish Women's Centre two of which are reproduced below.

Using human rights where resources are an issue

Case study 13 – Eighteen year old children in Irish Traveller families forced to leave home before permanent accommodation is given to the family.

Source: London Irish Women's Centre
Large Irish Traveller families are often placed in temporary accommodation for unacceptably long periods in London, sometimes for more than 10-15 years. Local authorities routinely say that this is because they have no large houses available for them. Often the families will be offered permanent accommodation after at least one of the children has turned 18, but they are told that the 18 year olds cannot live there (the 18 year olds are advised to make separate applications for housing elsewhere). This causes immense distress to the families involved, as they feel under pressure to force their older children to leave home, or to let them continue living with the family secretly. A London-based support organisation [LIWC] has regularly invoked the right to respect for family life to successfully challenge these decisions and to enable the families to continue living together, whether in their original temporary accommodation or otherwise.

LIWC successfully uses the Human Rights Act Article 8: The right to respect for private and family life, home and correspondence.

Using human rights to support family and private life
Case study 23 – Woman fleeing domestic violence able to prevent her children being taken into foster care
Source: London Irish Women's Centre

A woman and her children were fleeing domestic violence. The woman's husband was attempting to track the family down and they moved towns whenever he discovered their whereabouts. The family eventually arrived in London and were referred to the local social services department. Social workers told the mother that she was an 'unfit' parent and that she had made the family intentionally homeless. They said that her children had to be placed into foster care. An advice worker [from LIWC] helped the mother to challenge this claim on the basis of the right to respect for family life (protected by Article 8). As a result, the family were told that they could remain together and that the social services department would provide the deposit if they could secure private rented accommodation.

Typical issues

The following are typical issues which clients present to LIWC Advice staff who take up the issues with the relevant authorities or organisations and pursue to resolution:

Housing

Housing – LIWC has been contacted by Traveller families who have been put in temporary accommodation for over 10 years and are being constantly moved around because of poor conditions.

Homelessness – the authorities often find (that is, decide) Travellers to be "intentionally homeless" and therefore not a priority for re-housing. It is LIWC's experience that Travellers are more likely to be discriminated against. Travellers usually have to provide more information than others to the local authority as they are generally not believed.

Domestic Violence – (housing/homelessness) again women fleeing domestic violence are "found" to be "intentionally homeless" despite police and local authority policies encouraging women not to put up with abusive relationships. They are often not believed by the local authority housing department as there is a reluctance to involve the police in domestic violence issues and consequently there may be a lack of formal evidence.

Benefits
LIWC staff mainly assists with completing forms and carrying out benefit checks. The most common benefits applied for are disability living allowance and social fund applications.

Debt
There is a high proportion of debt incurred by purchasing goods from catalogues and loans raised especially to pay for travel costs - often to Ireland for weddings or funerals. LIWC also assists with increasing income via community care grants or charity grants.

When working with Travellers the main difference from the settled community is that there are usually multiple issues involved, gathering evidence can be problematic because of poor literacy levels and the constant moving around which makes tracking correspondence and follow-up difficult. Our staff also find that the cases tend to be more extreme so, in the case of domestic violence, the violence is more violent and more frequent.

LIWC Case Study of Ms C.
LIWC assisted in a Client (Ms C.) and her family being provided with temporary accommodation after fleeing domestic violence. A few years later the accommodation was cancelled by the local authority and because Ms C. refuses to take hostel accommodation she was found (they decided) intentionally homeless.
Problems faced – Ms C. does not read or write so was not fully aware of her rights and she should not have been "found intentionally homeless". By the time Ms C. came to

LIWC with her changing circumstances the decision could not be reviewed as it was outside of the time limits. LIWC assisted the Ms C. to present at another local authority and to obtain a new decision which can go to review. Ms C. was then referred to solicitor whom LIWC briefed. LIWC is also dealing with other issues for Ms C. which are particularly common among the Travelling community:

- Health Issues – it has been difficult for Ms C. to access health services as she was forced to be constantly moving between temporary addresses.
- Benefits – Ms C. was not receiving correct benefit entitlement and could be entitled to Disability Living Allowance.
- Children – Ms C.'s children were not accessing education, young peoples' services or appropriate benefits.

LIWC makes referrals to Social Services, Traveller education, GPs and solicitors to deal with housing issues. Because of the referrals inter agency work is required. Housing and benefit issues usually take much longer and are more complex and difficult when working with Travellers compared to the settled community. The structures in place are designed for the settled community and inflexible. Claimants are asked to provide a lot of information to the decision makers which is usually difficult for a Traveller to comply with. Because of the transient way of life documents get lost, births may not be registered, medical services are harder to access and not followed up, dates are forgotten. Low levels of literacy, especially among the older generation, means appointments can be missed, letters go unread and action not taken until too far down the line and severe penalties are threatening.

[4]

Legislation

The provisions of the 1947 Town and Country Planning Act, the 1959 Highways Act and the 1960 Caravan Sites Act all restrict the ability of Travellers to lead a nomadic life. The 1968 Caravan Sites Act was a mixed blessing but its better features were withdrawn when the Act was repealed in 1994.

Caravan Sites Act 1968
This Act addressed the need to make public provision for Travellers for the first time. However, it applied a non-ethnic definition of Travellers imposing a duty upon local authorities to provide adequate sites for all *"persons of a nomadic habit of life whatever their race or origin"*. It also contained discriminatory *"designation"* provisions.

The Act imposed a general duty upon London boroughs to provide a minimum of 15 pitches for Travellers but there was no time limit set to compliance. Furthermore, councils who met their quota of 15 pitches could then apply to the Department of the Environment (DOE) for "designated" powers to evict any "surplus" Traveller caravans that stopped within their boundaries.

To highlight the racism inherent in this practice, Sylvia Van Toen (Travellers Education Project) in *Hackney Race Equality* March 1990 points out: *"Imagine a law which restricts the number of Bangladeshi families ... to fifteen ..a borough"*.

Councils could also obtain designation status by satisfying DOE that they had no land on which to build a site or by persuading the department that it was unnecessary or inexpedient to make provision.

The Traveller population increased substantially in the last decades of the 20th century but, according to the Department of the Environment 62% of local authorities in England had failed to provide a sufficient number of pitches by 1992. Thus at least one-third of the community were forced to live on unauthorised sites; about 3,200 families according to Action Group for Irish Youth (AGIY) and London Irish Women's Centre (LIWC) research published in 1993.

Some authorities provided more than 15 pitches and operated non-harassment policies. However, by 1994, 26 out of 33 London boroughs had designated status. Some designated boroughs such as Islington and Westminster made no provision whatsoever and denied Travellers the right to stop anywhere in their Borough.

Many of the sites created under the 1968 Act were next to or on marginal space near rubbish dumps, busy main roads and industrial areas; often extremely hostile environments in which to live and bring up children.

The Westway, London

Thus, while the 1968 Act led to an increase in traveller site provision, particularly following the introduction of central Government funding for sites in 1978, it also assisted in the creation of *"no go"* areas for Travellers.

The designated powers of eviction available under sections 10 and 11 of the Act were followed by section 39 of the **1986 Public Order Act** which granted the police almost immediate powers of eviction. Additional powers of eviction against Travellers were introduced in the **1990 Environmental Protection Act** and the **1991 Planning and Compensation Act**.

The criminalisation of Travellers reached its peak in the **1994 Criminal Justice and Public Order Ac**t which effectively outlawed the Traveller way of life.

The 1968 Caravan Sites Act was repealed in 1994. The removal of the duty on councils to provide sites meant the construction of local authority sites came to a standstill.

Councils also ignored the new **Planning Circular (1/94)** that called upon councils to assist Irish Travellers and other Traveller groups to identify land they could buy and develop as sites themselves .

The 1994 repeal of the duty to provide sites created a profound shortage of sites resulting in an increase of unauthorised encampments (roadside) and a reluctant move into housing. Both have had a negative impact on Irish Traveller's health and education. The increase in unauthorised encampments also led to increased tension between Gypsies, Travellers and the wider community.

Some Irish Traveller families bought their own land to settle on so that they would not be constantly harassed to move on from the roadside. For those that applied for planning permission in advance, there was a 90% failure rate for Traveller applications - compared to 20% for the settled community.

With this experience, some bought and settled on land seeking to initiate retrospective planning applications many of which were turned down resulting in families being evicted from their own land.

The consequences have been that Travellers have been forced to move into housing or camp illegally. Living on unauthorised sites means living under constant threat of eviction, without ready access to education, health care and welfare services. Traveller women have often had to cook, clean and care for their families without access to electricity, water or sanitation.

The problems created by the lack of properly serviced sites not only fuelled the prejudices of the settled community who have blamed the Travellers for their living conditions but they have also undermined the health of this minority group.

The average life expectancy for Travellers in this country was 48 years according to Pahl and Vaile (1988). More recent studies continue to indicate very poor health, high infant mortality rates, low life expectancy and high hospitalisation rates.

Into the 21st Century

Since 2004 campaigns and increased community tensions have led to the introduction of a series of new policies.

In 2006 the Government announced the creation of a **Task Group**, initially with the remit of enforcement and with no community representation. After protests, one Gypsy and one Irish Traveller were included on the Task Group to look at site provision as well as enforcement.

The Group Report in 2007 led to the Government placing a statutory duty on local authorities to assess the accommodation needs of Irish and other Traveller groups.

The **Gypsy and Traveller Accommodation Assessment** made an attempt to gather the up-to-date data necessary for proper planning and decision making but there were problems with the piecemeal approach to this by different local authorities.

The results are being fed into regional spatial strategies and Regional Planning Bodies are determining how many pitches are needed within each authority in the region. The Greater London Authority consulted on its new Strategic Plan for London in 2009 and the conclusions drawn by the GLA indicate they propose to make a provision roughly 50% of that identified in the Needs Assessment – which in itself was considered an underestimation by organisations working with Travellers.

Planning Circular 1/06

This guidance note obliges local authorities to identify land in their Development Plans that is appropriate for Traveller sites. Such land is to be made available for Irish and other Traveller groups to purchase and develop their own sites. Some public provision could also be created as the Government enabled registered social landlords to apply to the Housing Corporation for funds to develop sites.

Where local authorities fail to identify suitable land, the Secretary of State has powers of intervention, including the right of directing local authorities to comply. Failure by the local authority to provide such land will also be a material consideration in the planning process, which may help retrospective planning applications by Gypsies and Travellers.

Having land identified is likely to have a significant effect on prices and may make it unaffordable for Travellers, who find it especially difficult to obtain mortgages from conventional lenders.

The Government made £56 million available for the **Gypsy & Traveller Site Grant** between 2006 and 2008. Prior to this an annual allocation of £8 million was all that was available. The grant could be used to renovate and refurbish sites as well as develop new ones. However, there have been few initiatives to involve tenants in the management of council owned sites which impacts negatively on their sense of belonging and security. This is further exacerbated by the system of rent regulation which means the housing benefit payable is less than the economic rent and most existing sites are now loss making. Previous poor practice has been recognised and the Government and Housing Corporation have more recently commissioned site design and management guidance.

Housing and Regeneration Bill 2007
This was introduced following a ruling in the European Court of Human Rights (Connors v UK). The UK Government response indicated that it will improve security of tenure on local authority Traveller sites.

The **Anti-Social Behaviour Act of 2003** created a provision where increased eviction powers could be used where Gypsies and Travellers can be directed to a vacant pitch. This could further marginalise Travellers because if they refuse to go to directed pitches they must leave the confines of a local authority and not return for three months. Any breach of this can lead to heavy fines and penalties. With so many of the existing sites being poor and inadequate there may well be a reluctance to move on as directed – leading to further tensions and insecurity for affected families. The Government hoped this policy may result in more transit sites being created by local authorities but opposition from the settled community makes it unlikely.

The **Race Relations Amendment Act 2002** places a duty on local authorities and other public bodies to outlaw racial discrimination; ensure equality of access to services and carry out consultation of ethnic minorities; all with the aspiration of maintenance of good community relations. They also have to consider the impact of policies on ethnic minorities by carrying out impact assessments; which should offer some protection to Irish Travellers as an ethnic minority. However, current legislation still falls short of placing a statutory duty on local authorities to provide and facilitate sites.

Greater London Authority

London boroughs, supported by the Greater London Authority (GLA) undertook the Gypsy & Traveller Accommodation Assessment as required by **Circulars 1/2006** and **4/2007** and followed this up with consultation on the replacement **London Plan** in 2009.

The conclusions reached included the view that as 72% of the need identified came from Gypsies and Travellers already in housing (rather than caravans) some of the solution to need should be found in bricks and mortar type accommodation. The report does not accept the argument that Travellers have a genuine aversion to living in bricks and mortar.

In January 2010 the report proposals for 538 new pitches to be made available between 2007 and 2017 were revised downwards to 268 (representations from Travellers argued for 807); the proposed 40 transit places were reduced to 29 and additional plots for travelling Show people lowered from 73 to 53. The revisions were open for consultation until 11 May 2010 and, at the time of writing this booklet the final conclusions had not been published. (See Appendix 4 p54)

APPENDIX 1:

Definition of Ethnicity

In 1983 the Court of Appeal stipulated 7 characteristics confirming ethnicity (of any group), the first two of which were considered essential criteria: [Mandla v Dowell 1983 2AC 548]

1. A long shared history of which the group is conscious as distinguishing it from other groups and the memory of which it keeps alive.
2. A cultural tradition of its own including family and social customs and manners, often, but not necessarily, associated with religious observance.
3. Either a common geographical origin or descent from a small number of common ancestors.
4. A common language, not necessarily peculiar to the group.
5. A common literature peculiar to the group.
6. A common religion different from that of neighbouring groups or from the general community surrounding it.
7. Being a minority or being an oppressed or a dominant group within a larger community, for example a conquered people (say, the inhabitants of England shortly after the Norman conquest) and their conquerors might both be ethnic groups.

APPENDIX 2:

Irish Travellers as a distinct Ethnic Group

The Commission for Equality & Human Rights and most local authorities recognise Travellers as an ethnic minority and have done so since the early 1980's [see Appendix 1] and the Swann Report of 1985.

The ethnic status of Travellers was further confirmed by another Court of Appeal ruling in 1989 in a case brought by the Commission for Racial Equality (CRE). This involved the licensee of the Cat and Mutton pub who had put up a sign saying *"NO TRAVELLERS"* in his pub in London Fields. The Court held that the term Traveller encompassed both Gypsies and other caravan site dwellers and that the "No Traveller" sign was indirectly discriminatory under the **1976 Race Relations Act.**

Not all Travellers are directly protected under Race Relations Law however. Those who have taken to the road in recent years, such as *"New Age Travellers"* cannot claim to have a long history of travelling life and, at the time of writing have not acquired ethnic status.

A series of court cases sought to exclude New Age Travellers by re-defining *"nomadic"* to include the concept of purposeful travel, economic independence and a tradition of travelling. This also has implications for many traditional Travellers.

APPENDIX 3: International Law

All Travellers can claim the right to lead a nomadic existence as a basic human right which is enshrined in international law. The **European Convention of Human Rights [ECHR]** and the **United Nations Covenant on Civil and Political Rights [ICCPR]** include several articles which are important for Travellers.

These include the rights of individuals to:
- have *"respect"* for their *"family life"* and *"home"* [**Article 8 ECHR**] and
- enjoy the basic rights and freedoms outlined in the ECHR *"without discrimination on any ground"* [**Article 14 ECHR**].

The **United Nations Charter Article 31** guarantees:

"Everyone ... the right to freedom of movement and residence within the borders of each state."

In February 1993 the British Government accepted the **Council of Europe's Recommendation 1203** on Travellers in Europe which noted that:

"Intolerance of Gypsies by others has existed throughout the ages. Outbursts of racial or social hatred, however, occur more and more regularly and the strained relations between communities have contributed to the deplorable situation in which the majority of Gypsies live today."

The proposals went on to recommend that:

"member sates should alter national legislation and regulations that discriminate directly or indirectly against Gypsies".

However, the **Criminal Justice and Public Order Act** (enforced 1994) was in direct contradiction of this.

Communal area at Springtime Close site in Southwark - the site is overlooked by a major South London police station

The Westway, Hammersmith London

APPENDIX 4: Site Provision

Gypsy sites provided by Local Authorities and Registered Social Landlords in England July 2009

	Total no. Pitches	Of which		Caravan Capacity
		Residential	Transit	
ENGLAND	**4837**	**4617**	**220**	**7956**
North East	218	218	0	321
North West	341	315	26	567
Yorks & Humber	539	512	27	958
East Midlands	259	257	2	449
West Midlands	525	506	19	851
East of England	877	850	27	1689
LONDON	**494**	**474**	**20**	**740**
South East	1020	989	31	1408
South West	564	496	68	973

Count of Gypsy and Traveller Caravans 16th July 2009

Numbers of Caravans	Authorised sites with planning Permission		Unauthorised sites (without planning permission)				Total All
			on Sites on Gypsies own land		on Sites on land not owned by Gypsies		
Region	Caravans Socially Rented	Caravans Private	"Tolerated"	"Not tolerated"	"Tolerated"	"Not tolerated"	Caravans
ENGLAND	**6603**	**7105**	**1205**	**987**	**579**	**958**	**17437**
North East	277	168	8	1	27	0	481
North West	520	644	27	46	31	147	1415
Yorks & Humber	832	476	118	13	52	91	1582
East Midlands	316	691	71	156	104	64	1402
West Midlands	698	774	143	91	8	52	1766
East	1358	1818	296	292	175	86	4025
LONDON	**665**	**46**	**73**	**25**	**0**	**0**	**809**
South East	1255	1604	214	238	35	125	3471
South West	682	884	255	125	147	393	2486
Average caravans per site :	21.4	4.7	3.6	3.4	4.3	5.5	6.2

Gypsy sites provided by Local Authorities and Registered Social Landlords in London 16th July 2009

	Total Pitches	of which are:		Caravan capacity	Date site opened	Date last site changes
		Residential	Transit			
TOTAL FOR LONDON	**494**	**474**	**20**	**740**	**1972**	**2004**
Barking and Dagenham	**11**	**11**	**0**	**15**		
Eastbrookend Dagenham Road Rush Green Romford RM7 0SS [2]	11	11	0	15	1979	2001
Bexley	**10**	**10**	**0**	**12**		
Powerscroft Road, Foots Cray Sidcup DA14 5DT [1]	10	10	0	12	1997	n/k
Brent	**31**	**31**	**0**	**31**		
Lynton Close, Great Central Way Neasden NW10 0JE	31	31	0	31	1970	2009
Bromley	**36**	**36**	**0**	**72**	**1990**	**2009**
Star Lane Orpington BR5 3LW	22	22	0	44		
Old Maidstone Road Sidcup DA14 5AY	14	14	0	28	1995	0
Camden	**5**	**5**	**0**	**9**	**1994**	**0**
96 Castlehaven Road NW1 8PU [1]	1	1	0	1		
105 Camden Street NW1 OHS [1]	4	4	0	8	1988	2008
Croydon	**19**	**19**	**0**	**19**		
Lathams Way Croydon CRO 4XP	19	19	0	19	1986	0
Ealing	**24**	**24**	**0**	**48**		
Bashley Road NW10 6TH[2]	24	24	0	48	1970	1997
Greenwich	**40**	**40**	**0**	**57**		
Thistlebrook Manor Way Abbey Wood SE2 9SQ [1]	40	40	0	57		
Hackney	**27**	**27**	**0**	**38**		
Abbey Close 1/7 Rendlesham Rd E5 8PA [1]	7	7	0	8	1996	2005
St. Theresa's Close Homerton Rd E9 5EF[1]	7	7	0	7	2008	2008

	Total Pitches	Resi-dential	Transit	Caravan capacity	Date site opened	Date last site changes
Hackney continued						
Palace Close Chapman Rd E9 5DW [1]	4	4	0	6	2008	2008
St Anthony's Close Wallis Road E9 5EH [1]	1	1	0	1	2008	2008
Eton Manor, Quarter Mile Lane E9 5FB [1]	8	8	0	16	2008	2008
Haringey	10	10	0	10		
Clyde Road, 116a - d Clyde Rd Tottenham N15	4	4	0	4	1985	1995
Wallman Place, 1-6 Wallman Place, Bounds Green Road N22	6	6	0	6	1986	1996
Harrow	1	1	0	1		
Watling Farm, Watling Farm Close Stanmore HA7 4UY	1	1	0	1	1975	2000
Hillingdon	40	20	20	55		
Colne Park, Cricketfield Rd West Drayton	40	20	20	55	1980	2008
Hounslow	20	20	0	20		
The Hartlands, Church Road Cranford	20	20	0	20	1970	2005
Kensington & Chelsea	20	20	0	38		
Westway, Stable Way Latimer Road W10 6QX [1]	20	20	0	38	1975	2004
Kingston upon Thames	15	15	0	15		
Swallow Park 172 Hook Rise North, Tolworth	15	15	0	15	1970	0
Lambeth	15	15	0	15		
Lonesome Depot Leonard Rd SW16 5TA [1]	15	15	0	15	1972	1997
Lewisham	3	3	0	3		
Thurston Road, 14 - 29 Thurston Road SE13 [1]	3	3	0	3	1975	n/k
Merton	15	15	0	15		
Brickfield Road Wimbledon SW19 8UJ	15	15	0	15	1972	2008

	Total Pitches	Residential	Transit	Caravan capacity	Date site opened	Date last site changes
Newham	15	15	0	30		
1-15 Parkway Crescent Stratford [1]	15	15	0	30	2006	0
Redbridge	17	17	0	17		
Northview, Forest Road Hainault IG6 3HW	17	17	0	17	1968	2002
Richmond upon Thames	15	15	0	28		
Bishopsgrove, Hampton TW12 1AP	15	15	0	28	1972	2009
Southwark	42	42	0	78		
Springtide Close, 1-5 Staffordshire Street SE15	5	5	0	10	1995	n/k
Burnhill Close, 1-6 Burnhill Cls Leo St SE15	6	6	0	6	1995	n/k
Brideale Close, Glengall Rd SE15	16	16	0	32	1993	2006
Ilderton Road, 21 - 49 Ilderton Road SE16 3JU	15	15	0	30	1986	2000
Sutton	15	15	0	34		
The Pastures, 80 Carshalton Road Banstead SM7 3DX	15	15	0	34	1993	n/k
Tower Hamlets	19	19	0	34		
Eleanor Street, Bow E3 4NP	19	19	0	34	1983	2001
Waltham Forest	17	17	0	34		
Peacocks Close, Folly Lane Chingford E4 8TX [1]	17	17	0	34	1985	n/k
Wandsworth	12	12	0	12		
Trewint Street SW18 4HD	12	12	0	12	1974	2003

Notes	
n/k	not known
1.	July 2009 count data estimated using July 2008 count data. Data not received from the following local authorities: Ashford, Basingstoke & Deane, Bexley, Boston, Camden, Canterbury, Crawley, East Lindsey, Elmbridge, Fareham, Fenland, Fylde, Gloucester, Greenwich, Hackney, Isle of Wight, Kensington & Chelsea, Lambeth, Malvern Hills, New Forest, Newham, Poole, Sheffield, Southampton, Spelthorne, Surrey Heath, Thurrock, Waltham Forest and Winchester
2.	The July 2009 Count was not done by the following authorities due to circumstances beyond authorities control: Barking & Dagenham, Ealing, Ipswich, Kingston upon Hull & Sedgemoor.
	Source for all tables - www.communities.gov.uk

GLA Assessment for additional needs for Gypsy & Traveller Pitch Provision 2007-17

Proposals sent out for consultation by the GLA in Autumn 2009 but likely to be changed downwards following "Minor Revisions" proposed in January 2010 for consultation ending May 2010:

Barking & Dagenham	14	Hounslow	16
Barnet	22	Islington	5
Bexley	27	Kensington & Chelsea	7
Brent	20	Kingston upon Thames	15
Bromley	58	Lambeth	10
Camden	6	Lewisham	15
City	0	Merton	9
Croydon	22	Newham	17
Ealing	26	Redbridge	12
Enfield	5	Richmond upon Thames	9
Greenwich	32	Southwark	15
Hackney	19	Sutton	10
Hammersmith & Fulham	5	Tower Hamlets	28
Haringey	25	Waltham Forest	11
Harrow	9	Wandsworth	10
Havering	42	Westminster	2
Hillingdon	22	**LONDON**	**538**

Resources

London Irish Women's Centre
www.liwc.co.uk   020 7249 7318

Irish Traveller Movement
www.irishtraveller.org.uk   020 7607 2002

London Gypsy Traveller Unit
www.lgtu.org.uk   020 8533 2002

Gypsy, Roma & Traveller History Month
www.grthm.co.uk

Travellers' Times
www.travellerstimes.org.uk

Federation of Irish Societies
(Information about all UK Irish organisations)
www.irishsocieties.org   020 7833 1226

London Irish Centre (Camden)
www.irishcentre.org   020 7916 2222

Irish Chaplaincy
www.irishchaplaincy.org.uk   020 7482 5528

Greater London Authority
www.london.gov.uk

British Institute of Human Rights
www.bihr.org.uk

Communities and Local Government
www.communities.gov.uk

London Irish Women's Centre

Advice, Information,
Counselling and Groups
for women of
Irish & Irish Traveller
birth and descent

Monday - Friday 9-5

59 Stoke Newington Church Street
London
N16 0AR

020 7249 7318
07794 663113 (Text only Advice line)
www.liwc.co.uk
info@liwc.co.uk

Registered Charity 1080966   Companies House 2287034